READ THIS BOOK TONIGHT TO HELP YOU WIN TOMORROW

ROB GILBERT, PH.D.
EDITED BY JOHN SIKES JR.

CHAMPIONSHIP PERFORMANCE
Charlotte, North Carolina

ISBN—13: 978—1482317794
ISBN—10: 1482317796

Read This Book Tonight to Help You Win Tomorrow

Published by Championship Performance
10612 D Providence Road Suite 262
Charlotte, NC 28277
Phone: (704) 321-9198
FAX: (704) 321-0203

Web: www.championshipperform.com

Book production by Elevita Media

All rights reserved. The reproduction of this work in any form whether electronic, mechanical, or other means including photocopying is forbidden without the written permission of the publisher.

This book is dedicated to:

DR. JOAN SCHLEEDE-HORN
and
DR. GEORGE HORN

In 1979 when I was fresh out of graduate school and beginning my career at Montclair State, Joan and George were incredibly kind to me. Joan was my chairperson and George was a fellow faculty member. In other words, Joan was "my boss" and George became a trusted colleague. I am so grateful that I met both of them when I did. Thank you, Joan and George!

CONTENTS

CHAPTER 1: The Best Athlete Never Wins   9
1A. Featured Quotes: Belief and Self-Confidence

CHAPTER 2: Overcoming Your Fears   21
2A. Featured Quotes: Overcoming Adversity and Fears

CHAPTER 3: Release Your Mental Emergency Brake   37
3A. Featured Quotes: Concentration and Focus

CHAPTER 4: Balancing Caring Too Much Versus Too Little About Your Performance   57
4A. Featured Quotes: Preparation and Performance

CHAPTER 5: The Gordon Thomas Story—"How to Play Out of Your Mind and to the Max of Your Ability"   69
5A. Featured Quotes: Enthusiasm and Passion

CHAPTER 6: The True Meaning of a Team Leader   77
6A. Featured Quotes: Mental Toughness

CHAPTER 7: The Difference Between a Winning and Losing Attitude   85
7A. Featured Quotes: Achievement

CHAPTER 8: Coaching Lists for Better Performance   91
8A. Featured Quotes: Determination

CHAPTER 9: 5 Rules for Going All Out including the Difference Between Decision and Action   99

CHAPTER 10: The List: 40 Power Statements to Help You Perform Your Best When the Pressure is On   105

CHAPTER 1
The Best Athlete Never Wins

Tommy Lasorda, the legendary manager of the Los Angeles Dodgers baseball team, had a secret weapon. Whenever he felt his team absolutely had to win a game, Lasorda used his secret weapon and the Dodgers almost always won.

In a little while, I'm going to tell you exactly what Lasorda's secret weapon was because the same thing that worked for Lasorda's Dodgers is going to work for you.

So let's get started . . .

I'm Dr. Rob Gilbert and for the last 34 years I've been teaching sport psychology at Montclair State University in New Jersey. Over the years, I've helped thousands of athletes just like you do their best when it means the most.

Tomorrow you have an important competition, tournament, match or game. Let me ask you four questions . . .

#1. Suppose you stay up all night tonight lifting weights. Will you be stronger tomorrow?

Of course not.

#2. Suppose you run all night. Will you be faster and have more endurance tomorrow?

Definitely not.

#3. Suppose you spend all night practicing. Will you be more skilled tomorrow?

Once again, no, no, no.

#4. BUT . . . can you have a better ATTITUDE tomorrow than you have right now?

Absolutely!

You can't improve your strength, speed or skill overnight, but you can improve your attitude. In other words, between tonight and tomorrow, you can go from a losing attitude to a winning attitude.

That's exactly what this book will do for you. This book will show you exactly what to do so you can . . .

HAVE THE MINDSET OF A WINNER.

But hold on!

If you want to have the mindset of a winner, there is one thing you absolutely cannot do.

There is one thing that will guarantee failure.
There is one thing that will destroy you.
There is one thing that'll rob you of any chance you have of winning tomorrow.

This one thing is . . .

YOU CAN NOT LOSE HOPE.

"Without hope, there is nothing."

BOB GIBSON — PRO BASEBALL PLAYER

Why? Because once you lose hope - you lose all your chances of winning.

If you feel it's hopeless because your opponent is so good - you'll lose.

If you feel it's hopeless because you're so bad - you'll lose.

Here's the truth: In sports, there are no hopeless situations.

My first job is

TO GIVE YOU HOPE.

Let me tell you a story about the greatest underdog of all time, WHO COULD HAVE LOST HOPE BUT HE DIDN'T.

It was way back during biblical times and David was to go on the field of battle the next day to fight a gargantuan named Goliath.

David was just about to go to bed when three of his friends came into his tent to make a condolence call. Basically, they told David that it was nice knowing him because they knew he was going to get killed the next day.

"Wait a second," David said. "You think Goliath's going to win?"

His friends nodded.

"No way," David said.

"How can you be so confident?" one of his friends asked.

"Simple. God is on my side. I have my slingshot and Goliath's so big — HOW CAN I POSSIBLY MISS!"

How was David able to be so positive?

How was David able to have so much hope?

Because he knew something you need to know.

David knew that . . .

THE BEST ATHLETE NEVER WINS.

I know this sounds strange, but stay with me, I'll explain.

Would you have bet money that David would beat Goliath? Of course not.

IT WAS A HOPELESS SITUATION.

Goliath was bigger.
Goliath was stronger.
Goliath was fiercer.

In other words, Goliath was better in every respect.

But he lost.

Why did he lose?

Goliath lost because even though he was better, David fought better.

You see . . .

THE BEST ATHLETE NEVER WINS.
THE ATHLETE WHO PLAYS BEST ALWAYS WINS.

It doesn't matter who is better — all that matters is who plays better.

It doesn't matter who is bigger — all that matters is who plays better.

It doesn't matter who is seeded or ranked higher — all that matters is who plays better.

THE PERSON OR TEAM WHO IS BETTER DOESN'T WIN.
THE PERSON OR TEAM WHO PLAYS BETTER DOES.

David was the first in a long list of winners who weren't "supposed to" win.

Have you seen the movie "Miracle" about the 1980 U.S. Olympic hockey team? They were "supposed to" lose to the invincible Russians. But the United States won. Why? Even though the Russians were the better team, the United States was the team that played better.

Here's a little piece of trivia . . .

Three days before the Olympic Games began in 1980, at an exhibition game at Madison Square Garden in New York City, the same two teams met. The Russians beat the Americans by a score of 10-3. Mike Tully, who covered that game as a sportswriter, guest

> "Always remember that Goliath was a 40-point favorite over little David."
>
> RALPH "SHUG" JORDAN — COLLEGE FOOTBALL COACH

lectures in my sport psychology courses. He says that the Americans were so outclassed that night they were lucky they didn't lose by a score of 20-0!

After that game, United States Coach Herb Brooks knew that his first job was not to let his team lose hope.

Ten days after that humiliating loss, the U.S. played the Russians for real in the Olympic tournament. Final score . . .

United States 4
Soviet Union   3

My first job is to give you the same type of hope that Herb Brooks gave his team.

My second job is to make sure you are the one who plays better tomorrow - so that you will win! Whether you're "supposed to" or not.

So starting right now, remember no matter who you are competing against, no matter what happens —THERE IS HOPE.

This acronym will help you to remember what we've just been talking about . . .

H.O.P.E. — Hold On Possibilities Exist

1A. Featured Quotes on Belief and Self-Confidence

"To be a great champion you must believe you are the best. If you're not, **pretend you are.**"
    Muhammad Ali — Professional Boxer

"If you believe in yourself, have dedication and pride and never quit —you'll be a winner. The price of victory is high, but so are the rewards."
    Bear Bryant — College Football Coach

"You have to believe in yourself when no one else will."
    Sugar Ray Robinson — Professional Boxer

"Experience tells you what to do. Confidence allows you to do it well."
    Stan Smith — Professional Tennis Player

"Believe you can and you're halfway there."
    Theodore Roosevelt — U.S. President

"Momentum is the most unstoppable force in all sports. The only way to stop it is to get in your own way or stop believing in yourself."
    Rocco Mediate — Pro Golfer

"You've got to take the initiative and play your game. In a decisive set, confidence is the difference."
Chris Evert — Pro Tennis Player

"There are no losers in sports, just winners and learners."
Brian Cain — Peak Performance Expert

"If my mind can conceive it, my heart can believe it, then I know I can achieve it!"
Jesse Jackson — Minister, Presidential Candidate

"Set daily, monthly, and long term goals and dreams. Don't ever be afraid to dream too big. Nothing is impossible. If you believe in yourself, you can achieve it."
Nastia Liukin — Olympic Gymnast

"Success is the peace of mind that comes as the direct result of self-satisfaction in knowing you have made the effort to become the best player you were capable of becoming."
John Wooden — College Basketball Coach

Chapter 2
Overcoming Your Fears

There are two other things that can destroy your performance tomorrow if you handle them wrong. They are WORRY AND FEAR.

I'll bet that one of the reasons you're reading this right now is that you're worried about what might happen tomorrow.

Right now I want you to write down, on the following blank lines, four things that worry you about tomorrow. Don't hold back. Write down your big worries and your small ones. Nobody will ever see this list unless you share it. Here's the trick: Don't think a lot about it — just write. So what's worrying you . . .

1._____

2._____

3._____

4._____

Here is something you need to know.

IT'S OK TO BE WORRIED!

(In other words, don't worry about being worried.)
EVERYBODY WORRIES.

What do most people worry about?

They worry about what people will say about them and they worry about what people will think about them.

Let me tell you a story about a young girl who couldn't care less about what others would say or think about her . . .

Nobody thought that she was the smartest fourth grader. And nobody ever said that she was the most musical, the most athletic or the most artistic. But this little girl was the world's most confident fourth grader. She thought she could do absolutely anything.

One day, the art teacher came into class and said, "Today you can paint, draw, or finger paint anything you want."

The world's most confident fourth grader shot her hand up into the air and asked, "Can I draw a picture of God?"

Through her chuckles, the teacher said, "Nobody's quite sure what God looks like."

With all the confidence in the world, the little girl said, "Oh, they will when I'm done!"

NOW THAT'S A WINNING ATTITUDE!

Tomorrow you have to do what this little girl did.

Care a little less about what other people will think about you.

Care a little less about what other people will say about you.

Just because you might feel worried doesn't mean you have to act worried. Act confident regardless of how you feel.

> "It is natural to feel anxiety when you compete. But you hide it. Show it and you are through."
>
> JOE GARAGIOLA—SPORTS COMMENTATOR

Let's face it, if a little fourth grader can do it — YOU CAN DO IT TOO!

So instead of worrying what people will think and what people will say about you, do what the little fourth grader did . . .

ACT CONFIDENT!

The secret is to be a good actor.

JUST BECAUSE YOU ARE WORRIED
DOESN'T MEAN
YOU HAVE TO ACT WORRIED.

Another way of saying this is . . .

IT'S ALL RIGHT TO HAVE BUTTERFLIES
IN YOUR STOMACH,
JUST GET THEM TO FLY IN FORMATION.

Right now I bet you can act like the most confident person in the world. Let me prove it to you. Suppose I offered you $1,000,000 if you could act superbly confident for the next 10 minutes. Could you do this? Of course you could.

So here is what I want you to remember:

#1. It's ok to be worried. Everybody worries.

#2. Just because you are worried doesn't mean you have to act worried. You can act confident regardless of how you feel.

But suppose you'd like to act confident, but there's something bothering you that's even worse than being worried . . .

YOU'RE NERVOUS ABOUT YOUR PERFORMANCE.

Listen to me — it's okay to be nervous. Some of the greatest athletes of all time did their best when they were scared to death. You can too.

I have a friend who has been working with professional boxers for years. He knows all the greats. Once I asked him if the great fighters like Mike Tyson, Lennox Lewis and Evander Holyfield are as confident in the locker room as they look when they're walking into the ring. My friend told me that before the fight these superstar athletes were scared to death. But when they leave the locker room and start walking to the ring, they're acting as if they are confident.

IT'S OK TO BE NERVOUS.
JUST DON'T ACT NERVOUS.

One of the greatest pro basketball players of all time was Bill Russell of the Boston Celtics. Before most games he was so nervous that he threw up.

SO IT'S OK TO HAVE PRE-GAME JITTTERS, just don't act nervous. Act confident.

If you're scared, frightened or even panicky — hold on, there is hope.

Just because you feel a certain way doesn't mean you have to act that way. This means even though you feel scared, you can still act confident.

ACT AS IF IT WERE IMPOSSIBLE TO FAIL
EVEN IF YOU ARE SCARED.
EVEN IF YOU DON'T BELIEVE YOU CAN DO IT.

DON'T LET YOUR FEELINGS DICTATE YOUR ACTIONS.
LET YOUR ACTIONS DICTATE YOUR FEELINGS.

Most people feel they have to be successful before they can start acting successful.

Absolutely false!

They have it backwards. First start acting successful then you will become successful.

Look at superstars like Michael Jordan, Tiger Woods or Olympic athletes. They started acting successful well before they were successful.

You don't have to be a champion to you start acting like one.

As a matter of fact, the sooner you start acting like a winner, the better. How about right now?

Let's look at it this way . . .

Suppose you're a basketball player and one day at practice, Michael Jordan showed up. You're tested against Jordan. Who do you think would run faster, jump higher and shoot better?

> "It's ok to be scared sometimes.
> Just don't let it dictate your actions."
>
> MICHELLE AKERS — PRO SOCCER PLAYER

Michael Jordan, right?

Michael Jordan can beat you on physical tests, BUT can you go back to practice and instantly choose to have the attitude, the intensity, and the effort of a Michael Jordan?

OF COURSE YOU CAN.

ATTITUDE, INTENSITY AND EFFORT ARE A CHOICE!

Losing mindset: I have to be a champion before I can start acting like a champion.

Winning mindset: I can start acting like a champion well before I am a champion. And I can start acting that way right now.

REVIEW

What can you do right now to maximize your chances of winning tomorrow?

We've covered four things . . .

#1. Have hope. Realize that in sports there are no hopeless situations — just athletes who act hopeless.

#2. The best athlete or team doesn't win. The athlete or team that plays best does.

#3. It's ok to be worried — just don't act worried.

#4. It's ok to be scared, frightened or even panicky — just don't act scared, frightened or panicky.

REMEMBER THAT STORY ABOUT TOMMY LASORDA'S SECRET WEAPON?

Let me tell you the rest of it . . .

When Dodgers manager Tommy Lasorda sensed that his players were losing hope, or they were worried or scared or too tense, Lasorda brought in his "secret weapon" . . .

A COMEDIAN NAMED DON RICKLES.

Rickles' routine is that he makes fun of people. He makes fun of the way they look, the way they act, the way they talk, etc. When he was in the Dodger locker room no one escaped his wrath. The more Rickles talked, the more the players laughed. Not only were they laughing, they were laughing at themselves! When Rickles finished his pre-game routine, the Dodgers weren't as worried. They weren't as scared.

HAPPY STORY:

When you laugh (you loosen up physically . . .)
When you loosen up physically (you lighten up mentally . . .)
When you lighten up mentally (you play better . . .)
When you play better you win more often.

SAD STORY:

When you are worried or scared (you tighten up physically . . .)
When you tighten up physically (you get uptight mentally . . .)

When you get uptight mentally (you play worse.)
When you play worse, you lose more often.

Right now you're probably saying, "But Gilbert, you haven't made me laugh yet."

You're right. I haven't. BUT have you noticed how many stories I've been telling you? My stories are going to have the same effect on you that Rickles' jokes had on the Dodgers.

Stories loosen you up just like jokes do.

When you finish reading this book, you'll be ready to win just like the Dodgers were.

And this book works for two reasons:

#1. After you finish reading it, you'll know what to do and you'll perform better. Just like David.

#2. Your opponents won't know any of this information and they will keep making the same old mental mistakes they've always made and it'll hurt their performance. Just like Goliath.

So all you have to do right now is to relax and keep reading.

"Fear promotes failure.
Humor controls fear."

TIM MCCARVER — SPORTS COMMENTATOR

2A. Featured Quotes on Overcoming Adversity and Fear

"Adversity causes some athletes to break and others to break records."
Unknown

"Life is like a book with many different chapters. Some tell of tragedy, others of triumph. Some chapters are dull and ordinary, others intense and exciting. The key to being a success in life is to never stop on a difficult page, to never quit on a tough chapter. Champions have the courage to keep turning the pages because they know a better chapter lies ahead."
Unknown

"Courage is being scared to death and saddling up anyway."
John Wayne — Actor

"The ultimate measure of a person is not where they stand in moments of comfort and convenience, but in moments of challenge and controversy."
Dr. Martin Luther King, Jr. — Civil Rights Leader

"Adversity creates heroes."
Picabo Street — Olympic Skier

"To dare is to lose one's footing momentarily. Not to dare is to lose oneself."
Soren Kierkegaard — Danish Philosopher

"I am willing to put myself through anything — temporary pain or discomfort means nothing to me. As long as I can see that the experience will take me to a new level. The only path to the unknown is through breaking barriers — an often painful process."
Diana Nyad — Long Distance Swimmer

"Let fear be a counselor, not a jailer."
Anthony Robbins — Motivational speaker

"Show me a guy who's afraid to look bad, and I'll show you a guy you can beat every time."
Lou Brock — Pro Baseball Player

"The most rewarding things you do in life are often the ones that look like they cannot be done."
Arnold Palmer — Pro Golfer

"The chance for great victories is created by the adversity you have to overcome."
Woody Hayes — College Football Coach

"Great courage is not the absence of fear, but rather the ability to fight through it."
Pat Summitt — College Basketball Coach

"Courage means being afraid to do something, but still doing it."
Knute Rockne — College Football Coach

"Never place a period where God has placed a comma."
Gracie Allen — Comedienne

"I've never known anyone to achieve anything worthwhile without overcoming adversity."
Lou Holtz — College Football Coach

"Comparison is the enemy of contentment. Be the best you can be. Don't worry about junk beyond your control."
Anonymous

Chapter 3
Release Your Mental Emergency Brake

Jim was an average high school student, but his rich uncle promised him an expensive sports car if he graduated with honors from college. As soon as school started in September, Jim became a "real" student. He had never done that before. Every time he felt like sleeping late, he got up early. Every time he felt like cutting class, he went to class. Every time he felt like hanging out with his friends, he went to the library and studied.

His first semester in college, he got all A's. He never did that before, even in grammar school.

To make a long story short, in four years of college, Jim got a few B's, and the rest of his grades were A's. He graduated summa cum laude — just like his uncle did.

The night he graduated, his parents threw a party for him. And just as his rich uncle promised, a brand new red Jaguar sports car was waiting for him.

After the party, even though it was late, Jim drove over and picked up his best friend Ray. Ray was really into cars. He was in awe of Jim's Jaguar. He took Jim to a drag strip like straight away, where the police never go, so they could see how fast the car could go.

Jim got the car up to 80 mph.

Ray said, "You don't know how to drive a car like this. Let me show you."

He got behind the wheel but couldn't do much better. A little embarrassed, Ray said, "This car should be able to go 170, there must be something wrong with it. You'd better take it back to the dealer tomorrow."

The next day when Jim drove into the dealership, he was greeted by the sales manager. When the sales manager heard the problem, he brought in the master mechanic.

The mechanic put the Jaguar up on the lift. He looked at the car for about a minute and then brought it down and turned to Jim and said, "You're the kid who got all A's in college, aren't you?"

Jim nodded.

"How long have you been driving?"

"Five years."

"Let's see if I got this right. You've been driving for five years and you're smart enough to get all A's in college, but you don't know that you don't drive a $75,000 sports car with the emergency brake on?"

HERE'S THE BIG QUESTION:
DO YOU HAVE YOUR EMERGENCY BRAKE ON?

You probably don't even realize you have an emergency brake.

You do.

Oh, it's not a physical one like in a car. It's a mental one.

Let me prove how destructive your mental emergency brake can be:

"The greatest danger for most of us is not that our aim is too high and we miss it. But that our aim is too low and we reach it."

MICHELANGELO — ARTIST

Do you ever perform better in practice than in competition? That's because you have your mental emergency brake on.

Do you ever get intimidated by an opponent or a team and play poorly? That's because you have your mental emergency brake on.

Do you ever lose to someone that you've easily beaten before? That's because you have your mental emergency brake on.

Look at all the thousands of hours you've spent practicing, working out, sweating and sacrificing. In just a few seconds, this mental emergency brake can destroy all your preparation.

DON'T WORRY!

YOU'RE GOING TO LEARN HOW TO RELEASE YOUR MENTAL EMERGENCY BRAKE SO THAT YOU CAN UNLEASH YOUR TRUE POTENTIAL AND PERFORM BETTER THAN EVER BEFORE!!!

Right now you might be asking why you haven't released this emergency brake before.

Simple.

You never even knew it existed.

It's impossible to control something that you didn't even know about.

Now that you know about it, you'll learn how you can control it.

Once you learn how to release your emergency brake, you'll be able to go all out without holding back.

Let me give you a quick example of how destructive this mental emergency brake can be.

Recently when I was walking to class, I saw one of my students who was scheduled to give a presentation that day.

He was walking to class having a lot of fun talking and joking with friends.

When he got into the classroom, he took a seat and had a relaxed conversation with the young woman sitting next to him.

During class, he was very articulate asking and answering questions.

But when it was time for his presentation, he was so stressed that he gave a terrible talk.

WHAT HAPPENED?

It all has to do with the mental emergency brake.

My student's mental emergency brake was OFF when he was walking to class.

His mental emergency brake was OFF when he was speaking to that young woman before class.

His mental emergency brake was OFF when he was asking and

answering questions.

But as soon as it was his turn to speak, his mental emergency brake went ON —full force. And it destroyed his talk.

Now let's assume this student was 20 years old. He has been speaking successfully his whole life. Thousand and thousands of conversations. Millions and millions of words.

After class I spoke to this student. He confided to me that he totally stressed himself out. I asked him why he was so stressed out. He said he felt he had to give a great talk so that he could get an "A."

In other words he did the two things that put his mental emergency brake on immediately:

He felt he had to give a great talk.
He focused on his grade.

I'm going to make sure you don't make these tragic mistakes . . .

So how are you going to make sure your mental emergency brake is released? You only have to do two simple things.

#1 HOW TO RELEASE YOUR MENTAL EMERGENCY BRAKE

EMERGENCY BRAKE ON: If you feel that you must win or if you feel you have to win - your mental emergency brake will be on. BIG TIME! Athletes don't perform well under this type of pressure.

"I have lost tournaments
by trying too hard."

DAVIS LOVE III — PROFESSIONAL GOLFER

EMERGENCY BRAKE OFF: If you want to win and you don't feel you have to win, you'll release your mental emergency brake immediately.

When you think to yourself, "I have to win" and "I must win," it creates tension. When you think, "I want to win," it reduces tension.

"I have to win" and "I must win" causes you to over react. "I want to win" helps you to under-react.

The change you can make ...

"I HAVE TO WIN TOMORROW."
              to
"I WANT TO WIN TOMORROW."

"I MUST WIN TOMORROW."
              to
"I WANT TO WIN TOMORROW."

If you feel you have to win, you're hurting yourself by putting too much pressure on yourself.

Just suppose you're holding a hose and you're trying to water your lawn. But you're doing one thing wrong — you are standing on the hose.

What will happen? The pressure in the hose will build up until it explodes!

That's what happens when you feel you must win or you feel you have to win. You're putting too much pressure on yourself and you'll eventually feel like you're going to explode.

Step off the hose.

Many years ago, I worked with one of the country's top female gymnasts.

She was one of the top until her senior year in high school. Her senior year started as a disaster. She was performing worse than she did her freshman year.

We finally figured out exactly what the problem was. Before each meet her senior year, her coach and parents would point out which college coaches were at the meet scouting her.

Her parents and her coaches created this "I have to win/I must win" mindset. This was putting too much pressure on the gymnast. She felt she had to impress the college coaches so that they would offer her a scholarship. This is a losing mindset.

There's a happy ending to this story. And here's one of the stories that this gymnast told me helped her get back to competing "like her old self."

Once upon a time, there was a young wrestler who was a champion. However, during his senior year in high school everything changed. Wrestlers he used to beat easily were now beating him. Tournaments he used to win, he wasn't even making it to the finals.

Needless to say, he was very upset. This was his senior year. Everyone thought this was his year to win the state championship.

Everyone expected him to get a full scholarship to one of the big wrestling schools.

One day his coach gave him a phone number of a sport psychologist.

He made an appointment.

At the first session, the wrestler told the sport psychologist all the pressure that he was under – from wrestling and selecting a college to his parents and girlfriend.

The sport psychologist taught the wrestler a simple relaxation exercise, which he did every single night. And he felt better almost instantly.

Within a week, he was his old self again. Within two weeks, he was wrestling better than ever before.

His coach was amazed with this dramatic turn around. The coach wanted to know what happened.

"Well, I went to see that sport psychologist. He taught me a very simple relaxation technique that I do every night."

"Can you tell me how you do it?" asked the coach.

"Sure," said the wrestler, "Every night before I go to sleep, I sit in

"To win, you must treat a pressure situation as an opportunity to win, not as an opportunity to fail."

GARDNER DICKINSON — PRO GOLFER

a chair and close my eyes for about 20 minutes and repeat a phrase over and over again."

"Would you be betraying any trust if you told me what the phrase was," asked the coach.

"No, not at all," said the wrestler. "I just sit in a chair, relax, close my eyes and repeat to myself over and over again, "I don't give a damn. I don't give a damn. I don't give a damn."

It wasn't that the wrestler didn't give a damn about how he was wrestling. It was that he didn't give a damn about what everyone was going to think and what everyone was going to say about him.

Maybe you might even want to try this technique.

Here's how you can reduce the pressure on yourself right now . . .

RULE #1. Realize there are NO must-win games.

If you're dreading tomorrow, it's probably because you feel like you must win.

RULE #2. There are no have-to-win games.

When you feel you must win or you feel you have to win — you are weak. When you want to win — you are strong.

"I must" and "I have to" create stress.

"I want to" creates energy!

When you feel you want to win, then you're in great psychological shape! You're not putting too much pressure on yourself.

HOW TO RELEASE YOUR EMERGENCY BRAKE

EMERGENCY BRAKE ON: Focus on Winning.
EMERGENCY BRAKE OFF: Focus on Giving a Full Effort.

First of all, let's talk about focus.

Oprah Winfrey once said, "Your focus is your future."

Almost every athlete focuses on the wrong thing.

Let me see if I can get you to focus on the wrong thing . . .

RIDDLE: Anna's mother has three daughters. One is named Penny, another is named Nickel. What is the name of the third daughter?

Did you think the answer is Dime, Quarter, or Half-Dollar? That's because you are focusing on the wrong part of the riddle.

If you focus on the first two words of the riddle, "Anna's mother," you realize that the third daughter's name is Anna!

Most athletes do the same thing. They're focusing on the wrong thing — winning.

This is a big mistake

Why?

Because you don't have control over winning. You do have control over your effort.

Gandhi once said, "Full effort is full victory."

FOCUS ON EFFORT NOT OUTCOME!

Dr. Alan Goldberg is one of the very best experts in peak performance in the country. In his talks and seminars, he tells the story of when he was a freshman at UMass-Amherst. He played #1 singles on the tennis team. At the end of the season, he was playing in the the Yankee Conference championship finals. This was a big deal for a freshman.

Alan easily won the first set. He only needed to win one more set to become the Yankee Conference champion.

Between the first and second sets, the officials starting setting up for the awards presentation ceremony. Alan saw the big, beautiful stainless steel bowl that would go to the singles champion. He started thinking how cool it would be to bring that trophy back to his dorm.

All of a sudden, he started focusing more on the prize and less on the next point.

He started focusing more on the outcome and less on the effort. Alan lost the next two sets.

The moral to this story — you can't keep one eye on winning and the other eye on the ball. It won't work.

"The problem isn't that you can't focus. You're always focusing. The problem is: Are you focusing on the right thing?"

DR. ROB GILBERT — PROFESSOR OF SPORTS PSYCHOLOGY

Let me give you another example. Suppose you're an actor and you have the lead in a Broadway show. It's opening night. All the critics are in the audience. As you're performing, you start wondering what the critics are going to write about you in the papers.

The more you focus on how well the critics think you're performing — the worse you'll perform.

You have no control over what the critics will write — you do have control over your own performance.

Keep your focus on your effort not the outcome.

LET'S REVIEW.

In order to release your mental emergency brake, here's what you can do right now . . .

DO NOT feel that you have to win.
DO NOT feel that you must win.
DO FEEL that you want to win.
DO NOT focus on winning.
DO focus on giving a full effort.

3A. Featured Quotes on Concentration and Focus

"We compete, not so much against an opponent, but against ourselves. The real test is this: Did I make my best effort on every play?"
    Bud Wilkinson — College Football Coach

"Focused action beats brilliance any day."
    Art Turock — Professional Speaker

"I would tell our offense not to worry about winning or losing. Just take one play at a time. Focus on that one play, when it's over – regardless of the result – put it behind you and focus on the next one."
    Vinny Testaverde — Pro Football Player

"Learn from everyone you can and never cease trying to be the best you can. But don't get caught up in the things you have no control over."
    John Wooden — College Basketball Coach

"I never hit a shot, even in practice, without having a very sharp, in focus picture of it in my head first."
    Jack Nicklaus —Pro Golfer

"I used a lot of visualization in terms of who I would be guarding and who would be guarding me. When I was walking down the street I'd imagine those individuals in front of me then I'd imagine going around them."
    Isaiah Thomas — Pro Basketball Player

"There is only one time that is important — NOW. It is the only important time because it is the only time we have power and control over."
    Leo Tolstoy — Author

"I visualized making big plays. I try to dream about making them so they can become a reality. Nine times out of ten something good happened during a game."
    Lito Sheppard — Pro Football Player

"When you don't care whether you win or lose, you play full out. Then you're really dangerous because you can win. If you don't care about the outcome and you're playing for the point right there, that ball right there, then you possess a lot more power. You are more dangerous than ever because your energies are not conflicted."
    Sally Huss — Professional Tennis Player

Chapter 4

Balancing Caring Too Much Versus Too Little About Your Performance

Let's tie this all together . . .

QUESTION:
Why does it hurt so much when you lose?

ANSWER:
Because you care.

Caring is a good thing.

In order to be a great athlete you have to care.

You've got to care to get to practice on time.
You've got to care to eat right and workout.
You've got to care to commit yourself to a sport.

BUT . . .

QUESTIONS:
Why are you worried?
Why are you scared?
Why do you feel you must win?
Why do you feel you have to win?
Why do you focus so much on winning?

THE ANSWER:
You care *too much*.

CARING IS IMPORTANT.
CARING TOO MUCH IS DESTRUCTIVE.

Herb Cohen is one of the world's top negotiators. His most recent book is titled *Negotiate This*! But here's the important thing. The subtitle is . . . <u>BY CARING, BUT NOT T-H-A-T MUCH</u>.

If you want to be a better negotiator, you can't care t-h-a-t much. If you want to be a better athlete, you can't care t-h-a-t much.

Let me prove it to you. Think of two people you know who are dating. In any romantic relationship, one person usually cares more about the relationship than the other person. Let me ask you this — who controls the relationship: the person who cares more or the person who cares less?

It's always the person who cares less. There is power in caring less whether you're talking about romance or sports.

Once you start caring too much, you start worrying too much. You start being too scared. You make the competition *too* special. You focus *too much* on winning.

Then what happens?

You don't play up to your potential.

DO YOU CRUMBLE WHEN THE CROWD ROARS OR SOMEONE SPECIAL COMES TO SEE YOU COMPETE?

Here is a quick story to illustrate this point. There was a young man who entered a dance contest and was really doing well.

Then he looked out into the audience and saw . . . ME!

> "The secret to winning any game lies in not trying too hard. Let effort flow out of present focus."
>
> TIM GALLWEY — PEAK PERFORMANCE AUTHOR

HE WAS ONE OF MY STUDENTS!

Almost instantly, he went from great dancer to average dance.

Almost instantly, he went from being graceful to being robot-like.

Almost instantly, he went from being totally uninhibited to completely inhibited.

WHAT HAPPENED???

The next time I saw him in class, I asked him.

He said he was having a great time, being really into it. Then he saw me and he started thinking, "What's Dr. Gilbert going to say to me when he sees me at school on Monday?"

In other words, he went from caring to caring too much.

As soon as my student saw me, he got too serious.

DON'T MAKE THE SAME MISTAKE MY STUDENT MADE

Tomorrow is important.

Tomorrow is not special.

Every time you practice, every time you play, every time you do anything with your sport — it's important. But it's never special. Athletes do not perform well when they think something is "special."

If you want to screw up any performance, just use these "fourteen killer words":

"This is it."

"It's now or never."

"It's do or die."

"There's no tomorrow."

These words make something special when it's only important.

When athletes make something special they perform worse.

Every time you compete – it is important.

<u>It's never special</u>.

Start thinking this way. It's the way a winner thinks!

There's a country and western song that makes this point perfectly.

In "Come from the Heart," Kathy Mattea sings. . .

"You have to sing like you don't need the money.
You have to love like you'll never get hurt.
You have to dance like nobody's watching.
You have to come from the heart, if you want it to work."

I know something about you — you are a totally motivated athlete! Otherwise you wouldn't be reading this book right now.

I know something else about you – sometimes you get too motivated — especially before a major competition.

Lots of people think if some is good, more has to be better.

This is dangerous. Here is a silly example. Suppose you have a headache. You take two aspirin and the headache is gone in 20 minutes. But would you take 20 aspirin to make the headache go away in two minutes? Of course not.

Instinctively, you know some is good, but more is not necessarily better.

Being motivated is good, being *too* motivated is not so good.

Caring is good, but caring *too* much is bad.

Making tomorrow important is good, but making tomorrow too important is bad.

WINNERS ARE MOTIVATED.... LOSERS GET OVERLY MOTIVATED.

WINNERS CARE... LOSERS CARE TOO MUCH.

"Sports are a lot like a love affair. If you don't take them seriously, they are no fun. If you take them too seriously, they can break your heart."

Arnold Daily — Sports Writer

WINNERS MAKE IT IMPORTANT...LOSERS MAKE IT *TOO* IMPORTANT.

Remember, sometimes less is more. Less tension will allow you to be more intense.

Here's the key:

BE INTENSE WITHOUT BEING TENSE.

Loosen up.

Go all out with everything in your being.

Play like this is the last game of your life.

It's amazing that you will perform better when you simply...

PLAY!

There are three types of athletes: pretenders, performers and players.

Pretenders show up physically. They compete with their bodies.

Performers are a step above pretenders. They compete with their bodies and their minds.

But players put it all together. They have the total package and mind, body and spirit. They have released their mental emergency brakes so they:

1) ARE PHYSICALLY INTENSE.

2) HAVE "EYE OF THE TIGER" MENTAL FOCUS.

3) ARE EMOTIONALLY ENERGIZED.

Pretenders and performers can't compete with players.

In the next chapter you'll read a story that defines what a real player is.

4A: Featured Quotes on Preparation and Performance

"The will to win is not as important as the will to prepare to win. Everyone wants to win, but not everyone wants to prepare to win. Preparing to win is where the determination that you will win is made. Once the game, or test or project is underway, it is too late to prepare to win. The actual game, test or project is the end of a long process of getting ready, in which the outcome was determined in the preparation stage. So if you want to win, you must prepare to win."
Bobby Knight — College Basketball Coach

"In playing ball, or in life a person occasionally gets the opportunity to do something great. When that time comes, only two things matter: being prepared to seize the moment and having the courage to take your best swing."
Hank Aaron — Pro Baseball Player

"When you go from being proactive to reactive, that's a problem. Performance suffers and your opponent gains the upper hand."
Andre Agassi — Pro Tennis Player

"One of the most important lessons I learned during my years as an NFL quarterback was to always have respect for any opponent you play, but never to fear them."
Terry Bradshaw — Pro Football Player

"You lose with potential. You win with performance."
Bill Parcells — Pro Football Coach

"Consistent winners play with both emotion and discipline."
Mark Messier — Pro Hockey Player

"People ask me 'what was going through your mind in the race?' and I don't know. I try and let my body do what it knows from training."
Ian Thorpe — Olympic Swimmer

"Discipline usually involves doing the things you don't want to do. I cannot tell you that having discipline will guarantee success, but I can tell you that the lack of it guarantees failure. Remember to take the journey step-by-step, moment-by-moment. There are no shortcuts."
Steve DeMasco — Martial Arts Champion

"No one can attain perfection. But you must chase the heck out of it. You will then achieve excellence in the process."
Vince Lombardi — Pro Football Coach

Chapter 5

The Gordon Thomas Story—How to Play "Out of Your Mind to the Max of Your Ability"

Here's a story about an athlete who was able to put it all together and go all out and do his best when it meant the most. This is the story of GORDON THOMAS.

This story is about an athlete unleashing his superman potential, but it's not about a college star, a pro athlete, or an Olympic champion. It's the story of a forth-string college halfback who rode the bench for almost his entire athletic career.

Many years ago, Gordon was a senior at a small college in Pennsylvania. He was on the school's football team for four years, but he never played even one down. His coach liked having him around because Gordon was the ultimate team player. Gordon was always the first one to practice and the last one to leave. Gordon was always "up," always encouraging everyone. As his coach said, "Gordon is the glue that holds this team together."

The Monday before the last game of the season was Gordon's last game as a senior. Coach got the tragic news that Gordon's father had died over the weekend. Coach called Gordon at home. Gordon rose above the tears to thank the coach for calling.

"Gordon is there anything I can do for you?"

After a long pause, Gordon said, "Coach, I won't be able to be at the game on Saturday. I need to stay home with my mom and my sisters, but do you think the team could say a prayer for my Dad before the game?"

Coach promised him that they would.

Now it was the day of the big game. Two hours before kick-off, the coach was in his office and there was a knock on the door. In walked Gordon with his uniform on.

"Why aren't you home with your family?" the coach asked.

"Coach, I just had to be here today. Is the team still going to say the prayer for my dad?"

"Of course we will," the coach said.

Then Gordon looked up and said, "Coach, could please do another favor for me?"

"Sure, anything."

"Coach, I want to start today."

"Start? You've never played a down in four years," the coach blurted out. Then he realized the promise he had just made.

Who knows why, but the coach had a soft spot in his heart for the kid who had just lost his dad. He figured that he'd put Gordon in for a couple of plays for the first set of downs and then take him out.

The coach kept his two promises. The team said the prayer and Gordon started.

The second play of the game, the quarterback made a mistake and gave Gordon the ball. He ran for 12 yards. The next play, Gordon got the ball again. He raced for 8 more yards.

"One big play can win a football game. No one has any idea when that one play is going to happen. Therefore, every player must go all out on every play."

VINCE LOMBARDI — PRO FOOTBALL COACH

Gordon played so well that the coach never took him out. He had the type of game that football players dream about. He rushed for almost 200 yards and he scored three touchdowns. He single-handedly won the game for his team.

Gordon was carried off the field on his teammates shoulders, After the handshakes from the fans, after the slaps on the back from his teammates, a couple of newspaper reporters started to interview him.

What a great story: Gordon's last game was his first game and it was one of the best games any player at his school ever had.

The interview was interrupted when one of the assistant coaches told Gordon that the head coach wanted to see him in his office.

"Coach, thanks for putting me in today."

"Gordon, I never dreamed that you'd play so well. What happened to you out there today?"

After a long pause, Gordon asked, "Coach, did you ever meet my dad?"

"No, son, I've never had the pleasure."

"Coach, the reason you never met my dad and the reason I played so well today are really the same reason. Coach, my dad was blind and today was the first day he could ever see me play."

5A. Featured Quotes on Enthusiasm and Passion

"If you think it's going to be difficult to be energized and passionate . . . imagine how difficult it's going to be to compete against someone who's energized and passionate when you aren't."
Dr. Rob Gilbert — Professor of Sports Psychology

"Success is going from failure to failure without loss of enthusiasm."
Winston Churchill — Prime Minister of England

"A player who makes a team great is more valuable than a great player."
John Wooden — College Basketball Coach

"The first thing is to love your sport. Never do it to please someone else. It has to be yours."
Peggy Fleming — Olympic Figure Skater

"It doesn't take athletic ability to hustle."
Bill Parcells — Pro Football Coach

"You've got to get to the stage in your athletic life where **going for it** is more important than wins and losses."
Arthur Ashe — Pro Tennis Player

"Passion is powerful . . . nothing was ever achieved without it, and nothing can take its place. No matter what you face in life, if your passion is great enough, you will find the strength to succeed. So put your heart, mind, and soul into even your smallest acts . . . this is the essence of passion. This is the secret to life. I play to win even though common sense should tell me that I no longer have a chance. Even when I have been playing at my worst, or when all the breaks have been going against me. I approach each new day, each new hole, as a glorious opportunity to get going again."
Arnold Palmer — Pro Golfer

"Enthusiasm is the special spark that makes the difference between the leaders in every field and the laggards who do just enough to get by. Champions take chances. Always remember, pressure is a privilege."
Billie Jean King — Pro Tennis Player

"Every great and commanding movement in world history is due to the triumph of enthusiasm."
Ralph Waldo Emerson — Poet

"I tell all my players – 'hey, you might not be as good as Michael Jordan, but there is no reason you can't play with as much effort and enthusiasm as he does. No matter what your talent level is, you can always play hard."
Rob Evans — College Basketball Coach

Chapter 6

A Story About the True Meaning of a Team Leader

On Thanksgiving, just about everyone in the small town went to the traditional high school football game. At half-time of the big game, the football team from 1985 was honored. They were the only team in the school's history to win a state championship. That Saturday night, the class of '85 had their 25th reunion. It was there that former teammates Jack and Leo finally got a chance to talk about the good old days.

They hadn't seen each other since graduation. Jack, the all-state quarterback, had gone on to become one of the most successful and powerful CEOs in the country. After Leo graduated from college, he returned home and became the minister of a local church.
"Leo, I want to thank you for making me the success I am today," the businessman said.

"Jack, stop pulling my leg!" the minister said with a laugh. "From what I've read, you run a huge corporation. I didn't have anything to do with that and we haven't seen each other in years."

"You never knew this Leo, but when we were in high school, I was incredibly jealous of you."

"Me? Jack, you were the golden boy. All the big-time colleges were recruiting you. All the girls wanted to go out with you. And your name was in the paper every day."

"That may have been true, Leo, but here's what you didn't know. Even with all my honors and awards, you had the one thing I always wanted the most. The guys on the team elected you captain. I may have been the star of the team, but you were the captain of the team."

"I never knew that you cared about that," Leo said.

"I certainly did! It bothered me so much that just before graduation, I asked Coach why the guys on the team voted for you — and not me. Coach told me something I've never forgotten. He said, 'Jack, you're the best player I've ever coached. Leo doesn't have the kind of the talent you have. But here's the difference. Jack, you were the best player **on the team**, but Leo was the best player **for the team**. You wanted to be the **best player** in the state while Leo wanted to make us the **best team** in the state.'"

"You know, Leo, it was tough hearing that from Coach," the CEO admitted. "He was being so blunt and I knew he was telling me the truth. I was **selfish** and you were always **selfless** and everyone knew it. Everyone could see it everyday at practice. That's why everyone voted for you. It's a lesson I had to learn and it's a lesson I've never forgotten. You see, Coach was right. The difference between us is that for me, it was all about '**ME**,' and for you, it was all about '**WE**.'

"After we graduated, I worked hard to become more like you. As a matter of fact, thanks to you, I was voted captain of my college team my junior and senior years. And what Coach told me also helped me to quickly climb the corporate ladder.

"The 'old me' would have wanted my company to be the best company **in** the world," Jack said. Now I strive to make my company the best company **for** the world. Leo, that's why I need to thank you."

"I want to thank you too, Jack," the minister said warmly.

"A true leader has the confidence to stand alone, the courage to make tough decisions and the compassion to listen to the needs of others. He or she doesn't set out to be a leader, but becomes one by the quality of actions and the integrity of their intent."

H. Ross Perot — Business Executive

"For what?," asked Jack.

"You just wrote tomorrow's sermon for me!" replied Leo.

6A. Featured Quotes on Mental Toughness

"When I get tired and I want to stop, I'd wonder what my next opponent was doing. I'd wonder if he was still working out. I tried to visualize him. When I could see him working, I'd start pushing myself. When I could see him quit, **I'd push myself harder.**"
    Dan Gable — Olympic Wrestler and Coach

"It's not whether you get knocked down, it's whether you get up that counts."
    Vince Lombardi — Pro Football Coach

"Toughness is in the soul and spirit, not in the muscles."
    Alex Karras — Pro Football Player

"If you want to be successful, find someone who has achieved the results you want and copy what they do and you'll achieve the same results."
    Tony Robbins — Motivational Speaker

"A lot of track athletes run to see who is the fastest. I run to see who has the most guts."
    Steve Prefontaine — Olympic Runner

"The harder you work, the tougher it is to surrender."
Vince Lombardi — Pro Football Coach

"I don't run away from a challenge because I am afraid. Instead, I run toward it because the only way to escape fear is to trample it beneath your feet."
Nadia Comaneci — Olympic Gymnast

"If you're going though hell — keep going."
Winston Churchill — Prime Minister of England

"What counts in battle is what you do once the pain sets in. Gold medals *are not* really made of gold. They're made of sweat, determination, and a hard-to-find alloy called guts."
Dan Gable — Olympic Wrestler and Coach

"The most mature players are the ones who can handle success. When things go well, there is a tendency to relax. You can never let up if you are going to reach the highest levels of performance."
Dom Capers — Pro Football Coach

"Life is 10 percent what happens to you and 90 percent how you respond."
Lou Holtz — College Football Coach

Chapter 7
The Difference Between a Winning and Losing Attitude

The loser is almost always part of the problem. The winner is almost always part of the solution. Losers focus on the problems. Winners focus on possibilities. When confronted with a problem, losers get frustrated. When confronted with a problem, winners get fascinated.

The loser says, "That's not my job."

"The winner says, "Let me do it for you."

The loser sees a problem for every answer.

The winner sees an answer for every problem.

The loser focuses on the sand traps near the green.

The winner focuses on the green near the sand traps.

The loser says, "It's difficult."

The winner says, "It's not difficult, it's just time consuming."

Losers make promises.

Winners keep commitments.

Your <u>thoughts</u> determine what you want.

Your <u>actions</u> determine what you'll get.

I am 100% responsible for how I choose to respond to everything that happens in my life!

"Success is peace of mind which is a direct result of self-satisfaction in knowing you made the effort to do your best to become the best that you are capable of becoming."

JOHN WOODEN — COLLEGE BASKETBALL COACH

"Only those who dare to attempt great things—even if they fail—can ever achieve greatly."

ROBERT F. KENNEDY — PRESIDENTIAL CANDIDATE

7A. Featured Quotes on Achievement

"High achievement always takes place within a framework of high expectations."
    Motivational sign (ISC Gymnastics, Matthews, NC)

"Unfortunately, many great human potentials are lost when people dismiss big dreams as foolishness. We simply don't give our dreams time to take root in our minds. Too quickly, we cover them with a blanket of doubt and they are forgotten. I embraced my dream and took ownership of it."
    Ozzie Smith — Pro Baseball Player

"I'm not afraid to fail. I'm afraid to be mediocre."
    Junior Seau — Pro Football Player

"No one can give you the title of team leader. The title must be earned. The only way you can become a leader is if, one, you have a vision and two, you have a plan to get there."
    Lou Holtz — College Football Coach

"To be consistent you must be able to describe what you do as a process. The secrets of success are hidden in the routines [processes] of our daily lives. Accept the challenges so that you can feel the exhilaration of victory."
    George S. Patton — U.S. Army General

"For anything worth achieving, there is a price to be paid. To become dominant in any endeavor, can only be bought at the price of practice, training and discipline. The world is full of people who missed their destiny because they were not willing to pay the price. We are what we repeatedly do. Excellence, then, is not an act, but a habit."
Aristotle — Philosopher

"As long as you put in the work, you can own the dream. When the work stops, the dream disappears."
Jim Dietz — College Crew Coach

"I maintain my edge by staying a student – you always have something to learn."
Jackie Joyner-Kersee — Olympic Runner

"Create a definite plan for carrying out your desire, and begin at once, whether you're ready or not, to put it into action."
Napoleon Hill — Author

"Champions are champions not because they do anything extraordinary, but because they do ordinary things better than anyone else."
Chuck Noll — Pro Football Coach

CHAPTER 8

Coaching Lists for Better Performance including the 6 Best Motivational Sayings

Coach Bill Snyder's Eight Rules for Success

1. Improve every day as a player, as a person, as a student.

2. Care about your teammates, friends, and family.

3. Show great effort and enthusiasm.

4. Associate with only quality people.

5. Expect more of yourself, always.

6. Do it right, don't expect less.

7. Be genuine.

8. Make discipline a way of life.

Coach Pat Summitt's Definite Dozen

1. Respect yourself and others.

2. Take full responsibility.

3. Develop and demonstrate loyalty.

4. Learn to be a great communicator.

5. Discipline yourself so no one else has to.

6. Make hard work your passion.

7. Don't just work hard, work smart.

8. Put the team before yourself.

9. Make winning an attitude.

10. Be a competitor.

11. Change is a must.

12. Handle success like you handle failure.

Coach Vince Lombardi's Nine Most Important Rules:

1. Play to your strengths.

2. Work harder than anybody.

3. Be prepared to sacrifice.

4. Be mentally tough.

5. Know your stuff.

6. Act, don't react.

7. Keep it simple.

8. Focus on fundamentals.

9. Chase perfection and you'll run into excellence.

"People of mediocre ability sometimes achieve outstanding success because they don't know when to quit. Most people succeed because they are determined to."

GEORGE ALLEN - PRO FOOTBALL COACH

Dr. Gilberts Six Favorite Motivation Sayings

1. Shoot for the moon. Even if you miss, you'll be among the stars.

2. If it is to be, it is up to me. (The 10 most powerful two-letter words)

3. The will to win is not nearly as important as the will to *prepare* to win.

4. Things work out best for those who make the best of the way things work out.

5. It's the start that stops most people.

6. Losers make *promises*, winners keep **commitments**.

8A. Featured Quotes on Determination

"Champions are not made in a gym. Champions are made from something deep inside of them: a desire, a vision, a dream to be the best."
Muhammad Ali — Pro Boxer

"I attribute my success in life to this: I never gave up or made excuses."
Florence Nightengale — Founder of Modern Nursing

"Persistence is what makes the impossible possible, the possible likely and the likely definite."
Robert Half — Founder, Robert Half Internation

"The difference between the impossible and the possible lies in a person's determination."
Tommy Lasorda — Baseball Manager

"The highest compliment you can pay me is to say that I work hard every day and that I never dog it. Goals provide the energy source that powers our lives. One of the best ways we can get the most from the energy we have is to focus it. That is what goals can do for us: concentrate our energy."
Denis Waitley — Motivational Author and Speaker

"It's important to push yourself further than you think you can go each and every day — as that is what separates the good from the great."
    Kerri Strug — Olympic Gymnast

"Excellence is not *expected* effort – it is *extra* effort."
    Ed Tseng — Peak Performance Expert

"Push yourself time and again. Don't give an inch until the final buzzer sounds."
    Larry Bird — Pro Basketball Player

"Being your best is not so much about overcoming the barriers other people place in front of you as it is about overcoming the barriers we place in front of ourselves. It has nothing to do with how many times you win or lose. It has no relation to where you finish in a race or whether you break world records. But it does have everything to do with having the vision to dream, the courage to recover from adversity and the determination never to be shifted from your goals."
    Kieren Perkins — Olympic Swimmer

"What lies behind you and what lies ahead of you is not nearly as important as what lies within you — that inner determination to be the best."
    Oliver Wendall Holmes — Poet

"Hard work beats talent because talent doesn't work hard."
Tim Tebow — Pro Football Player

"The price of success is dedication, hard work and an unrelenting devotion to the things you want to see happen."
Frank Lloyd Wright — Architect

"Persistence can change failure into extraordinary achievement."
Matt Biondi — Olympic Swimmer

Chapter 9

Rules for Going All Out including the Difference Between Decision and Action

Persistence = Hanging on until you catch on.

Here are the five steps to persistence. If you use them, you'll never fail. Oh, you might fail in the short run, but you'll never fail in the long run.

Persistence is a simple process:

#1. What is the next step?

#2. What's in the way of taking that step?

#3. Remove or ignore the obstacle.

#4. Take the step.

#5. Go back to **#1.**

Rule #1. K - A = 0 (Knowledge without Action equals Nothing). It's worthless if you know what to do, but you don't do what you know.

Rule #2. Winners go all out. Losers hold back.

Rule #3. It's much better to go all out and lose than to hold back and win.

Rule #4. Get turned on by difficulties. Don't get frustrated — get fascinated!

Rule #5. Going all out can't be a some-of-the-time thing - it must become an all-the-time thing.

Here is a riddle before we finish, then I'm going to give you some closing assignments to do before you compete tomorrow.

Question: There are three frogs sitting on a log. One frog decided to jump off the log. How many frogs are left on the log?

Typical Answer: Most people think the answer is "two". That's logical. Three minus one equals two. Logical, but wrong.

Correct answer: Three. There are three frogs sitting on a log. One frog *decided* to jump off the log. Just because the frog decided to jump doesn't mean it did jump. There is a huge difference between decision and action.

Message: There is a big difference between deciding to use the techniques we've been talking about and actually using them.

Final Thoughts: There are two more things I want you to do:

1) Read the list in Chapter 10 tomorrow morning (the day of your competition).

2) Get some sticky red dots and place them where you can see them tomorrow. Put a dot on your tennis racquet, equipment bag, water bottle or anything else you can think of that you will bring to your competition. No one else will know what they are for.

These red dots will be your own personal peak performance reminders of what we've covered here. Every time you see one of

"A lot of athletes are like ten speed bikes. There are many gears they have never used."

ANONYMOUS

these red dots, it will trigger your mind to think like a champion.

You know what Coke and Pepsi are, but why do Coke and Pepsi advertise every day constantly on radio, television, magazines, billboards, and the web? Because they know you need constant and continuous reminders to buy their product.

If Coke and Pepsi know how powerful advertising is and spend so much money on it, maybe you should advertise for yourself. These red dots will be your own personal advertisements to help bring out the best performance that lies within you!

CHAPTER 10
THE LIST—
40 Power Statements to Help You Perform Your Best When the Pressure is On

WARNING: DO NOT READ THIS FINAL LIST UNTIL THE DAY OF YOUR COMPETITION.

"You were meant to be here.
You were born to be hockey players.
This moment is yours!"

HERB BROOKS — USA HOCKEY COACH
(Final pre-game pep talk in the locker room before the 1980 U.S. Olympic Hockey team shocked the Russians in one of the greatest upsets in sports history.)

1. The best athlete doesn't win — the athlete who plays best does.

2. "Success is the peace of mind that comes as the direct result of self-satisfaction in knowing you have made the effort to become the best player you were capable of becoming." — *John Wooden*

3. "You're attitude more than your aptitude will determine your altitude." — *Lou Holtz*

4. You can change your attitude quicker than you can change your strength, speed, or skill.

5. "Keep HOPE alive." — *Jesse Jackson*

6. Doubt your doubts.

7. "Adversity creates heroes." — *Picabo Street*

8. Remember: Goliath was heavily favored, but David beat him.

9. "Where do you find motivation? You find it within yourself." — *Michael Jordan*

10. H.O.P.E. = Hold On, Possibilities Exist.

11. It's ok to be worried. Just don't be worried about being worried.

12. You can do your best even when you feel your worst.

13. If you're not nervous, you're not ready.

14. Just because you are worried doesn't mean you have to act worried.

15. Some of the greatest athletes of all time did their best when they were scared to death.

16. "The coward and the hero feel the same fear. They just react differently." — *Cus D'Amato*

17. "The hero is no braver than the ordinary man. But he is braver for five minutes longer." — *Ralph Waldo Emerson*

18. "Great courage is not the absence of fear, but rather the ability to fight through it." — *Pat Summitt*

19. "The chance for great victories is created by the adversity you have to overcome." — *Woody Hayes*

20. "Fear no opponent. Respect every opponent."— *John Wooden*

21. The only place success comes before work is in the dictionary.

22. The greatest pleasure in life is doing what people say you can't do. — *Walter Bagehot*

23. You can choose to have the attitude and intensity of a Michael Jordan.

24. When you loosen up physically, you lighten up mentally.

25. Once you release your mental emergency brake, you'll perform better than ever before.

26. "I have to win" create tension. "I want to win" creates energy.

27. There are no <u>must-win</u> games.

28. Focus on effort, not outcome.

29. "You have to get to the point in your athletic career when going for it is more important than wins and losses." — *Arthur Ashe*

30. "Full effort is full victory." — *Gandhi*

31. "I watched hours and hours of Michael Jordan on tape. He never relented for a second. He never backed down. He was on all the time." — *Brendan Francis*

32. "Make the total effort even when the odds are against you." — *Arnold Palmer*

33. "To give anything less than your best is to sacrifice the gift." — *Steve Prefontaine*

34. Don't be careless. Care less.

35. Be intense without being tense.

36. The 14 killer words:
    "This is it."
    "It's now or never."
    "It's do or die."
    "There's no tomorrow."

37. "Keep in mind that hustle makes up for many a mistake."
—*John Wooden*

38. Don't let up when ahead. Don't quit when behind.

39. "Winning isn't imperative, but getting tougher in the fourth quarter is. Always finish strong." — *Coach Paul 'Bear' Bryant*

40. "Play like a champion today." — *Sign in the Notre Dame Locker Room*

"It's kind of fun to do the impossible."

WALT DISNEY

Read This Book Tonight to Help You Win Tomorrow

Additional Book Order Form

1 copy: $25   **2 to 3 copies:** $22 each.   **4 to 9 copies:** $20 each
   10 to 19 copies: $15 each.   **20 or more:** $12 each.

# of copies_____   Order total_____

❏ Check enclosed. (Please make payable to: Championship Performance)

❏ Charge my credit card:

❏ Visa ❏ Master Card ❏ American Express ❏ Discover Card
Acct number:_____
Expiration date:_____

❏ Bill my organization. (Paperwork and PO # must accompany order — no exceptions.)

Ship to:
Name:_____
Organization:_____
Address:_____
City:_____
State_____Zip_____
Email Address:_____

**Return to: Championship Performance
10612 — D Providence Road, Suite 262, Charlotte, NC 28277**

Or order by phone: (704) 321—9198 or fax: (704) 321—0203

Order online at www.championshipperform.com

Another Great Book from Championship Performance

WINNING THE ATHLETIC MENTAL GAME

Get the Success Secrets of America's Top Coaches

In *Winning the Athletic Mental Game*, 21 of America's most successful coaches and 12 of the most respected performance psychologists offer their very best insights on what it takes to win in today's competitive environment. The interviews in the book come from coaches who have produced over 50 combined national titles. The performance psychologists have helped thousands of athletes reach their full potential as players.

Just a few highlights in the 33 chapters include:

- Lou Holtz: Essentials of Coaching Leadership
- Herb Brooks: Miracle Motivation
- Urban Meyer: Quickly Changing the Team Culture
- Suzanne Yoculan: Visualizing Success Leads to 9 Titles
- Frank Lenti: Maximum Motivation for the High School Athlete
- David Marsh: Turning Dreams into 12 National Titles
- Sue Enquist: Instilling a "Go for It" Spirit to Produce Champions

To read three sample chapters and a complete listing of all 33 chapters, please visit us online at:
www.championshipperform.com/winning-the-athletic-mental-game-2

- Order toll free by calling 1—877—465—3421 or…
- Online at www.championshipperform.com

Made in the USA
Charleston, SC
26 January 2014